WHEN LEARNING IS TOUGH

Kids Talk About Their Learning Disabilities

Cynthia Roby

Photographs by Elena Dorfman

Albert Whitman & Company • **Morton Grove, Illinois**

Special acknowledgment to the wonderful children whose experiences and insights are at the heart of this book. Thank you to Joe Folan, Andrew Hogue, Emily Keegin, Cameron Rodriguez, Mandy Seals, Uri Smith, Michele Wong, Lily and Alexis Williams, and of course, to my son Nick Roby, whose resilience and positive spirit in the face of his learning problems inspired this project. Thanks to my editor, Judith Mathews, for her steady support and impeccable guidance. And thanks to Elena Dorfman for her sensitive photos.   Cynthia Roby

Library of Congress Cataloging-in-Publication Data
Roby, Cynthia.
    When learning is tough: kids talk about their learning
disabilities / Cynthia Roby; photographs by Elena Dorfman.
        p.   cm.
    Summary: Children describe their learning disabilities,
talents, learning techniques, and misconceptions associated
with learning disabilities.
    ISBN 0-8075-8892-X
    1. Learning disabled children–United States–Juvenile
literature. [1. Learning disabilities.] I. Elena Dorfman,
ill. II. Title.
LC4705.R63 1994
371.9–dc20   93-6532
                                                 CIP
                                                  AC

Text is Trump Medieval Roman.
Design by Karen A. Yops.
Text copyright © 1994 by Cynthia Roby.
Photographs copyright © 1994 by Elena Dorfman.
Published in 1994 by Albert Whitman & Company,
6340 Oakton Street, Morton Grove, Illinois 60053-2723.
Published simultaneously in Canada
by General Publishing, Limited, Toronto.
Printed in the United States of America.
10 9 8 7 6 5 4 3 2 1

Fall seven times, stand up eight.
Japanese proverb

INTRODUCTION

Someday when you are at school, take a look around your classroom. Count out ten kids. Chances are that at least one of these girls or boys has a learning disability. More than two million children in the United States do. Maybe *you* do.

What does it mean to have a learning disability? It means that even though you may be perfectly smart, with average or above-average intelligence, learning is tough. You might have trouble in school with things like reading, writing, spelling, or math.

If you have learning problems, it sometimes seems as though your brain is playing tricks on you. And that's why classroom work can be so hard. But the good news is that you *can* learn. You just need to be taught differently.

All sorts of famous, super-successful people have learning disabilities: movie stars like Cher, Whoopi Goldberg, and Tom Cruise; athletes like Bruce Jenner and Greg Louganis; inventors like Albert Einstein and Thomas Edison; artists like Leonardo da Vinci and August Rodin; and Woodrow Wilson, the twenty-eighth president of the United States.

There are all kinds of learning disabilities. No two people have exactly the same learning problems. Most of these problems have long technical names. But whatever your learning problem is called, it might feel as though it takes a long time to get a message from your brain to other parts of your body.

Some people have trouble with visual perception, which means their brains confuse what they see. Maybe you mix up your letters or numbers or see them backwards. Sometimes this kind of learning problem is called dyslexia. Other people have problems with auditory perception, which means their brains have trouble understanding what they hear.

Some kids with learning problems have behavior problems, too. Some are hyperactive; they can't seem to sit still in class or to pay attention. This is called attention deficit disorder. Other kids are forgetful and disorganized. But just as you can get help with your schoolwork, you can get help with your behavior.

The purpose of this book is not to describe all the different learning problems people can have. It's to tell you how other kids with learning problems feel. You'll see that they probably feel a lot like you. Learning problems are problems that can be solved. Remember, you *are* smart even when you are feeling dumb. Just listen to the eight kids—all between nine and thirteen years old—who speak through this book. They are working hard and doing fine. And, most importantly, they are following their dreams.

Uri

In my old school, I was always in trouble....
I just knew there was no hope there. Then we
moved and I went to a new school, and they
got me right on the ball.

I am in the third grade. I have a twin brother named Uera. We're different looking: he's taller and thinner than me. We get along sometimes, but we usually do things separately.

My mom's a station agent for the Muni buses in San Francisco. She sits there all day and gives out transfers. I don't like her job, but I like my mom because she buys me toys and pepperoni pizza. My dad does plumbing. I have an older sister who has a baby son.

I never believed I would be in a book. I am so excited! God gave me a little bit of a learning problem, and now that problem has given me a little bit of luck.

I love swimming. I took swimming lessons last summer. By the time I quit I was on the advanced level. My brother was still on the beginner level—learning to go underwater and stuff. He has trouble with the water; he doesn't like it.

I have taken tae kwon do for a year and a half. It's a martial art. It has taught me a lot about myself and given me discipline. If someone on the street tried to hurt me, I would use my moves on them. I'd use the kicks, roundhouses, and upper punches that I have learned. But you never play with tae kwon do; you always take it real seriously.

I was seven when I started having trouble with my schoolwork. I was going to a different school at the time, a private school. In my old school, I was always in trouble. My mom detected my problems but the school couldn't help me. I just knew there was no hope there. Then we moved and I went to a new school, and they got me right on the ball.

They put me in a special ed. class, and it is fun.
You would wish that you could go there. We have a
bank. We do work in this big workbook and get lots
of points, and then we get fake money for the points.
Every Friday is bank day, and we can spend our money
on real things—we can buy real treats!

There are two girls and three boys in my class.
There used to be tons of boys and no girls—except for
the teacher. One of the boys doesn't do anything. All
he does is run around the school. I tell him, "You're

going to be a bum. And when your birthday comes, your mother isn't going to throw you a party." But *my* behavior in class is excellent.

One time a boy, who is in a regular classroom, said that our class was for retarded people, and I said, "No it's not. It's to teach us what we don't know." But most people don't make fun of my learning problems. My girlfriend is very understanding. She loves to hear me read.

Now it's beginning to feel like nothing is too hard for me. Well, some of the books, like the dictionary, are still hard. I'm getting really good at math. I just zoom through it.

I know I am just going to love high school because you don't have to stay at school all day. You can go out to lunch or something. I know the work will be hard, but I am going to try my best.

I want to go to college. I want to be a movie star, so I am going to study acting. If that doesn't work out, I am going to be a doctor or lawyer. But I really want to be a star.

> **Uri's Tip:** I want to tell other children with learning problems to do their best and if they don't know something, to ask somebody to help them.

Joey

I went through a long stage of thinking I was stupid. Mom would always tell me that I wasn't. Now I realize that I am not.

I have always been a pretty good artist. I just won the Mothers Against Drunk Driving poster contest in our county. I also love to paint landscapes in acrylics. I want to go to New York City for art college. When I grow up, I will be an artist. Or maybe I'll be a museum curator and preserve old art.

My mom is a housewife. She is a great cook. My dad works hard, too. I have two brothers—one older and one younger. We fight about everything.

I have four guinea pigs—two boys and two girls. They're so cute. One of the females has just had seven babies. They need to be with their mom for about four weeks after they are born, and then I'll sell them to a pet store.

I realized I had learning problems when I was in first grade. I was writing real slowly, and everyone else was writing real fast. Math was hard, too. I sort of knew there was a problem, but I didn't really understand it. It took me a long time to tie my shoes. My dad finally taught me. He didn't get too frustrated, but he had to tie my shoes until I was about eight.

When I was younger, I went through a long stage of thinking I was stupid. Mom would always tell me that I wasn't. Now I realize that I am not. That's because Mom kept telling me that over and over again. And my parents always remind me they love me, no matter what.

I don't think my learning problem has got a name. It just feels like part of my brain is locked or that there is a brick wall between some of the cells. It doesn't have anything to do with my intelligence. Not to brag, but I don't ever worry about being dumb anymore.

For some reason I have always known a lot of things that people don't learn in school. I've always been smart about things outside of school. Sometimes Dad will say, "I don't understand this," and I can explain it to him. For the past two years, sixth and seventh grades, I have gone to a school for kids with learning disabilities, and that has helped me do better in school.

I have learned to keep my binder really well organized, with all of my papers where they should be. I keep a list of what homework I have to do each night and have set up a routine that helps me remember to bring home everything that I need.

Kids can be really mean. One day last summer, my friend and I were at the pool. A couple of girls were lounging around and said, "Aren't you Joey? Aren't you that stupid kid who couldn't learn? Do you know how to spell 'the' yet?" I just blew it off. I think people like that are jerks. If they only knew how hard I work, they might understand. You just gotta stay tough and go with the flow. It's hard, but my work will be rewarded—I think.

If I am not an artist when I grow up, I might be a

priest or maybe a pilot. My learning problems might get in the way of my being a pilot because of the math. I think I may just be dreaming. Or I might like to be a teacher. If I were a teacher, I would always praise the kids on how they are doing. I always feel better when people compliment me. I would try to be very kind and explain things to my students. And I wouldn't make things boring.

My parents don't love me any less because I have a learning problem. They always remind me that they love my brothers and me. We are a family, no matter what.

Joey's Tip: As far as learning disabilities go, I say don't give up. You just have to work hard. Believing in myself has helped a lot.

JOE FOLAN to Nick

Michele

*When I was in my old school, I felt a little bit
mad about having a learning problem.
I couldn't read the words and the other kids
could....It made me feel really happy when I
finally got extra help.*

My apartment is above a video store in the city.
I can go right downstairs and rent a movie. I don't
have any brothers or sisters. My mother is Korean.
She works at a cafeteria. My dad works at the airport;
he's Chinese. We eat lots of Korean and Chinese food.
I like rice and noodles. I love pizza, too.

My favorite toy is my Cricket doll that I got one
Christmas. It talks and tells stories. I also collect
teddy bears. I have lots in my room. My favorite bear
is one my mom got me when I was a little baby.

I think my parents found out I had a learning
problem when I was two. I had a problem when people
would read to me. I would just draw on the books
because I couldn't understand the stories. It was hard
for me to understand the words.

I hated my old school. I went there through third grade. It was hard for me to do the work, so I would start fooling around. I had to go to the principal's office a lot because I was always talking in class. Then the school would call my parents.

When I was in my old school, I felt a little bit mad about having a learning problem. I couldn't read the words and the other kids could. I had to be sent to a quiet room so I could read. Somebody would help me there. It made me feel really happy when I finally got extra help. It didn't make me feel bad to go to the special classroom.

Then a few years ago, my parents decided to send me to a special school for kids with learning disabilities. I like it there, and the teachers help me. They treat me nicely and help me with my reading. Even so, recess is still the most fun. I run around the playground with the girls.

My parents help me with schoolwork. My dad used to show me flash cards. He still helps me with my math, my reading, and my spelling. He made a list

of all the math facts I have to learn; it's taped next to my bed. My parents are good to me. They don't get angry at me because I have learning problems.

I think my cousin may have learning problems, too. He is just little. He goes to school, and when the teacher reads a book he won't listen. He is like me at that age.

I'm good at art. I like to do self-portraits and paint and do projects. I would rather paint all day instead

of doing math or reading. I like classical music. And last year I learned to play "Can-Can" on the keyboard. I practiced every day. Sometimes I would mess up a little. Then I would do it over again, and I would do it right.

I think high school will be hard, very hard. I am going to study biology in college—it's all about human beings and the body parts. I'll be a teacher when I grow up. I will tell the kids not to fight or pinch. I want to teach little kids. They're cute!

Michele's Tip: I would tell other kids with learning problems to get books and keep trying to read them.

Andrew

*In the beginning when school was so tough,
I thought I might be retarded or somewhat
dumb....When I found out I had a learning
disability, I felt a little bit better because
I knew it wasn't my fault that I was
doing badly.*

I live in a house on a lagoon. I just got a kayak for my birthday. It was pretty easy to learn how to use it. I lived at the beach when I was little, and I have always liked the water. I learned how to swim early. It was very natural for me.

I love to play video games. They're fun, kind of fast, and exciting. I like the competition, and you can play with your friends.

My mom teaches at a local college, and my dad has a furniture company. My mom really tries to help me out. When I am real tired and having problems with my homework, she'll try to explain things quickly so I can get to bed.

In the beginning when school was so tough, I thought I might be retarded or somewhat dumb. That made me feel bad, naturally. When I found out I had a learning disability, I felt a little bit better because I knew it wasn't my fault that I was doing badly. But I still would have liked to be the same as other kids.

In second grade, I went to a new school and really felt like I was dumb or something. I was always put in the lowest group, and nobody liked me. The teacher thought I was stupid or not trying. She would never believe me when I said I couldn't do it. She'd say, "You can do it. It's just that you don't want to."

As soon as I was tested and we found out I had learning disabilities, I started going to a special school for kids with learning problems. It was right in the middle of third grade. I didn't feel good about it because it meant something was wrong with me. But it was better than staying at my old school, where the teachers didn't help me at all. It was also better because I wasn't all alone. One teacher there really understood learning problems. She was strict, but she understood. I really liked that. You couldn't learn much at the special school, but you could learn how to learn.

My learning problem is called dyslexia, although that is a really general term. Understanding concepts and memorizing things are difficult for me. It takes me longer than it takes most kids. Fortunately, my intelligence is not affected by my learning disability.

I still have trouble sometimes—with science, especially. I get B's and C's, but it's really hard not to blank out during a test. I get nervous, especially if there is a time limit and I have to get information down real quickly. That's why I'm glad that if you have a documented learning problem you can take as long as you want on some very important tests. When

I take the SAT's, I can take a day or two if I want.

The computer is helpful, especially if it has a spell checker. That really helps out. My papers almost look as though a secretary typed them. I think I will use a computer all through school if I learn to use the keyboard. Right now I am just a hunt-and-peck typist, so it takes me half an hour to do half a page.

It feels bad when someone makes fun of me because of something like my bad spelling. I say to myself that they are just being jerks. They really don't know who I am. I just try to put it aside. If they treat me like that when they need to borrow a dollar from me someday, I won't lend it to them.

As tough as school is, I want to go to college and get a good education and a good job. I probably want to go to business school. Or I might become an architect. I have a drafting table at my dad's house, and I really like to make drawings of houses, make them professional looking.

Andrew's Tip: One of the tricks I have is to try and stay as organized as possible. This really helps me because I am not thumbing through a whole bunch of papers trying to find my English paper or something. I also try to keep my binder as empty as possible so when I'm finished with papers, I put them in a big crate that I have at home.

Cameron

Having a learning problem like dyslexia is like fighting a constant battle, except in this case I have a very puny enemy. I can squash it like King Kong!

I was born on May fifth, Cinco de Mayo. My dad is Puerto Rican. A friend gave us a plaque for Christmas with our name—Rodriguez—on it. It is really cool. My background goes all the way back to Spain. But my mom's parents were from Czechoslovakia. I guess you could call me a tossed salad.

My dad is a lawyer, and my mom is a bookkeeper. My brother is in high school; he's sixteen. He sort of annoys me. I guess that's a teenager's job. Sometimes we play computer games or "Dungeons and Dragons," but we rarely do that anymore now that he's in his teenage twilight zone. Both my mother and my brother have slight learning problems, too.

Two or three months ago, I decided to become
a vegetarian. I just can't stand the idea of eating
anything that has had its own thoughts. I would love
to experience things the way animals do. Dolphins
are supposed to be really smart. Even though I am an
animal, I have no idea what an animal like a dog or
a whale or a dolphin experiences.

I found out I had learning disabilities when I was
in third grade. My teachers noticed I had been making
certain mistakes so I went to RSP—the Resource
Specialist Program—where they gave me some tests.

A little while later my parents told me I had dyslexia. I was surprised, but I wasn't depressed or anything. It's a mild case. It really woke me up to the world around me. It showed me that I was vulnerable.

I stayed in the Resource Specialist Program for three years. There were four or five kids there. My first teacher was the best. When she was there I felt like I didn't even have dyslexia! She had these weird games that we would play. In one exercise, we had to spin a ball, concentrate on it, and say the alphabet backwards. That was good for my eye-hand coordination. It was cool, and I think it really did help me.

Now I am in a regular sixth-grade class, and we do a lot of writing. Spelling doesn't matter that much because I have a spell checker on the computer.

That's the most wonderful thing because I don't have to keep looking words up in the dictionary. Sometimes when I am reading, my eye will mix up two letters in the middle of a word. But generally, I can read any word unless it is really long and weird. I just break it into syllables.

Math affects me, too. If I am writing down two numbers, I can mix them up and the problem is thrown off. I should always double-check my work, but I don't.

I usually don't study for tests because I find that if I study I don't get as high a grade. I get tired and scared

when I cram myself with knowledge. I have a pretty good memory without studying.

I am a very hands-on person. That's the way I learn best. I do a lot of building. I've repaired a gate at our house that was affected by an earthquake. I've also repaired our doorbell.

With every disadvantage, there is an advantage. I think the advantage I have is that I have a mild degree of psychic ability. I have ESP. The day of the earthquake in San Francisco, I said, "It sure feels like there is going to be an earthquake." That's happened maybe seven times in my life. Sometimes I've pictured people in my mind and then seen them on the street. I've thought, "Oh that's so freaky!"

I have never really felt embarrassed about having learning problems, although I don't go out and tell everyone I have dyslexia. I know I am smart. My learning problems have nothing to do with my basic intelligence. Having a learning problem like dyslexia is like fighting a constant battle, except in this case I have a very puny enemy. I can squash it like King Kong!

> **Cameron's Tip:** I consider my learning problem a challenge. The worst thing you can say is, "I am disabled and worthless." The best thing you can be is yourself. You should never try to change that.

Mandy

I suppose having a learning problem is okay,
but if I had one wish it would be that I could
be a regular kid with no learning problems.

My home is in the city. I have a younger brother and an older sister. We get along so-so. My mom works at the post office. She's a nice mom; she buys me clothes and takes me to the movies. My dad works as a security guard and at the post office, too. He takes me bowling and watches me do track.

I go to track meets, and I won a first-place ribbon in the eight-hundred-meter race. Running is something I do well, and it's fun. My school has a triathalon every year, and I am one of the fastest runners in it.

I started bowling last winter. I bowl with a team. There are three boys, and I am the only girl. I am the anchor on the team, the one with the highest average. My best score is 191.

I like to draw a lot. I also like collecting trolls. My favorite is my bowling troll. It has a shirt that says, "Strike" on the front and "I Love Bowling" on the back.

I found out I had a learning disability when I was quite young. I had trouble with reading. The letters looked upside down. I hadn't gotten my glasses yet, which made things even worse. It was kind of embarrassing because the other kids knew how to read. My friend Clarissa and I both didn't know how to read so we had to stay in second grade when everyone else moved on to third grade. It made me feel mad.

I don't know what my learning problem is called. I guess it just means I have a hard time learning. I suppose having a learning problem is okay, but if I had one wish it would be that I could be a regular kid with no learning problems.

One time—it was for a family party—we went to a restaurant. I couldn't read one of the words on the menu so I asked my sister to help me. A couple of kids at the table made fun of me for not being able to read well. That really upset me. I got up and walked away and sat in a corner. My sister came and said, "What's the matter?" She listened to me and made me feel better.

Later, I told my mom about what happened and she said, "They shouldn't have made fun of you.

Maybe they do better in school but they aren't as nice as you are. Remember the things you are good at, like sports."

For the past three years, I have gone to a special private school for children with learning problems. I have three teachers in my class now, and I am really learning. For example, I know a neat trick that helps with addition. I write the numbers from one to twenty in a row. Then if I want to do seven plus nine, I count to seven and then count nine more and get the right answer. Now that I am further along in math, I know another trick that helps me remember adding with nines. If you want to add nine and four, just put a one in front of the four which gives you fourteen, and take away one. Your answer is thirteen. Nine plus five is fourteen, nine plus six is fifteen, and so on.

I know more tricks for other school subjects. We use the code word *case* to help us remember what to put in our writing. *C* is for character; *a* is for action; *s* is for setting; and *e* is for emotion. All these tricks help.

I'm not looking forward to high school because I'm worried I might not do well enough and they'd hold me back again. I'm going to college even though my mother told me I'd have to dissect a frog. I hate bugs and lizards and frogs.

I think I'll get married someday. My husband will be nice, kind, have a sense of humor, and be gentle. And he won't take drugs.

I love running. My dad knew I would be a runner even when I was little. I ran in my walker, and when I was older, I always ran around when we went to the movies. We lived outside the city then, and I would run in the fields and grass. I love the feeling of the wind in my face and hair. At school, I've won the Presidential Fitness Award three times. I want to be in the Olympics. I would train hard, since practice makes perfect.

Mandy's Tip: I hope that kids who read this book realize that even if other people are better in math or reading, everyone can do something well. Don't worry about your learning disability!

Emily

*My biggest dread was that I was going to have
to stay back and repeat a grade.*

I guess you could say that my personality is
smack dab in the middle of my two parents'. My
mother, who is an artist and designs greeting cards, is
very overprotective. My father, who is a lawyer, is
more carefree. They don't care that I have learning
disabilities; they totally understand. Both of my
parents have, maybe not learning disabilities, but
different ways of learning. And they are not wonderful
spellers. My whole family is that way.

I have two sisters. My older sister isn't home
much now. My younger sister can be fun to be with.
Other times I want to kill her. For fun I like to hang
out with my friends downtown and look in stores but
never buy anything.

Music really gets my spirits up. I play the trumpet.
It's actually kind of hard to play, but it is easier for me
because I have musical experience from playing the
piano. I also love art. If I were painting a tree I might
put some pink and purple in it, or some blue, just to
make it more interesting. I've written tons of stories
this year, and I love poetry. But it has been hard for me
because I can't spell as well as the other kids.

When I first started school, I thought I must just
be dumb. Why shouldn't I be learning this stuff?

Sometimes I would even spell the word *in* wrong.
I would spell it *en*. I thought, "I am so stupid!" For
hours sometimes I would cry in my room. People
would say, "You are not stupid. You're wonderful."
and I'd say, "Yeah, right!" Now I know my learning
problems don't have anything to do with my basic
intelligence.

> **Reading**   by Emily Keegin
>
> *When I read I feel the words*
> *Wash around my head*
> *Like music of a butterfly*
> *A flower starting to grow*
> *I read of adventure*
> *Mysteries too*
> *Sports and poems*
> *So can you*
> *I go to my room*
> *sit upon my bed*
> *and feel the*
> *music wash around*
> *my head.*

When I was younger, I started falling further and further behind. In the fourth grade, when I started going to a tutor, I didn't tell any of my friends. Some kids whispered, "She's going to a tutor," and then it seemed like everyone found out and said to me, "Oh, gosh. Is she nice?" and stuff. I didn't really care what the other kids thought because I knew that was what I needed. After a time some other kids started going, too. The tutor was great and really helped me.

My biggest dread was that I was going to have to stay back and repeat a grade. I thought that would be really awful. Kids I knew who had stayed back lost all their friends and had to make new friends. Everyone thought they were stupid. Fortunately, I didn't have to stay back after all.

I've had a lot of testing and have found out that if I hear something I do a lot better than if I just see it. If you say six plus six equals twelve, or whatever, I keep saying it to myself and hearing it, and then I start remembering it. I learn from my ear, from hearing. Sometimes I make up rhymes to help me remember things like multiplication tables.

I usually know what's going on in school but sometimes I don't get concepts. I would like to tell my teachers, "Teach more by talking to me than by giving

me lots of pieces of paper and telling me to read them and to know things by tomorrow."

When I do my homework, I try to be really organized and work at my desk, but I usually end up propped against my bed. When I study for exams, I go over old tests. History comes naturally. In math, I just have to go over and over the problems until I know them.

After I finish school, the learning disabilities won't be as much a part of my life. Computers will help me with any written work. They already have spell checkers, and by then we will probably be able to talk to a computer and it will type.

I can't wait until I am about twenty-six or thirty, especially if I am doing something like art or if I am some kind of a superstar. I'm in plays at school, and I love acting. If I am an actress, the learning difficulties won't matter as much because I could listen to the script and then repeat it.

I have lots of ideas about what I want to be when I grow up. I will be slightly tall, like my Dad. I would like to be some kind of wonderful star. An actress, an artist, or a writer. I love history, so I might be an historian. I'd love to be some kind of sports person or maybe just do sports as a hobby. I love putting things together so I might be a model maker, doing something like models of houses. I'd like to be a designer. Interior designing is my favorite. I've decorated two doll houses. It's hard to decide right now. I've gone through so many ideas.

Emily's Tip: Recently, I've been putting my spelling words on tape and listening to them every night until I go to bed. That way they kind of get stuck in my head.

Nick

*I think you would call my learning disability
"the kids-who-learn-slowly" disease. It's
not like chicken pox. You don't have spots
on your body. It's just that you learn slowly.*

I was born in Hong Kong. My family was living
there because my dad was working for an American
bank that had an office in Hong Kong. We moved back
to the United States when I was just a baby so I don't
remember it at all. My mom is a writer.

I have one older brother; he's seventeen. I like it
when he hangs out with me and talks Mom into
taking us out for pizza. We definitely fight, though,
because it bugs me when he roughhouses with me.

I have two guinea pigs. They are always cuddled
up together in their cage. My dog is one of my best
friends. We got her from the Guide Dogs for the Blind.
She follows me around the house and sleeps in my
room at night.

My bedroom is cool because it's got great hiding places, clothes all over the floor, and a long shelf totally covered with a Lego town. I followed directions for some of it, but I designed most of the buildings myself.

I'm not very good at sports so I do volunteer work at a retirement home instead. It's through a program called "Love Is The Answer." Betsy is my special friend at the home. I thought I was going to get an old lady in a wheelchair who was about a hundred years old. But not Betsy! She walks faster than I do. We play dominoes with a ninety-nine-year-old man. I really like being with them a lot.

I think you would call my learning disability "the kids-who-learn-slowly" disease. It's not like chicken pox. You don't have spots on your body. It's just that you learn slowly.

My preschool teacher guessed that I might have a learning disability because of some of the trouble I had drawing things. My parents had me tested and found out my brain has a hard time understanding information. Everyone tells me I'm smart, and, especially when I am talking to grown-ups, I know I am. I guess I'm different, maybe unique. For two years, I went to a special school for kids with learning problems, but for most of my life, I have gone to a regular school and gotten extra help from a tutor.

I bump into my learning disabilities in pretty much every subject. In reading, a *b* will turn into a *p* sometimes. And then sometimes the word *god* will turn into *dog*. Sometimes I feel like people don't understand exactly what I am trying to say. I can't get out the right words.

This year I have learned how to outline a story by finding the most important words when I am reading. Outlining helps me organize my thoughts. When I write, I know I have to read everything back to myself very slowly. I check the spelling, punctuation, handwriting, and grammar. Math is really hard for me. I go really, really slowly. The numbers seem to jump around on the page. In long division, I use a

system of arrows to make sure I am putting all the numbers in the right place.

Most of all, I need to be organized, otherwise I get sloppy and forget things. When I get home, I write what I have to do for homework—spelling, math, whatever—on my pen board. I also write down my household chores—doing the garbage, things like that. I label every drawer with what's in the drawer— paper, envelopes, pens, pencils, old files. I even have a drawer for goldfish food.

Other kids can be mean if you have a learning

problem. The worst thing happened one summer when I went to day camp. After swimming we had to line up by grade to get on the bus, so I got in the right line—the fourth-grade line. I'm pretty short for my age, so these boys I didn't know said, "You look like you're six. Are you really in fourth grade?" When I said, "Yes," they said, "Okay, then what's ten times ten?" When I didn't know the answer it made me feel real bad. Short and dumb!

But I don't think a learning disability is the worst thing that can ever happen to someone. I think it would be worse if I couldn't walk or couldn't see or couldn't talk.

I might want to be a teacher. I would like to teach kids with learning disabilities. Because I have learning problems, I will understand some things that other teachers don't. I would know what the kids are going through. Some kids think they are totally stupid. I'd make sure they understand that having a learning disability doesn't mean you're dumb. It just means you learn differently.

Nick's Tip: Kids should remember that there are tons of people out there with learning disabilities. Don't ever, ever worry that you are different. My personal motto is: Suffer, survive, and move on.

Cynthia Roby is a journalist and oral historian and is a board member of the San Francisco Marin County chapter of the Learning Disabilities Association.

Resources for Parents of Children with Learning Difficulties

National Center for Learning Disabilities
381 Park Avenue South
Suite 1420
New York, NY 10016
212-545-7510

Learning Disabilities Association
of America (LDA)
4156 Library Road
Pittsburgh, PA 15234
412-341-1515
(Chapters in most states)

The Orton Dyslexia Society
Chester Building, Suite 382
8600 LaSalle Road
Baltimore, MD 21286-2044
410-296-0232
(Chapters in most states)

Other Organizations That Can Help

American Bar Association
Center on Children and the Law
1800 M Street NW #2005
Washington, D.C. 20036
202-331-2250

American Speech–Language–
Hearing Association (ASHA)
10801 Rockville Pike
Rockville, MD 20852
800-638-8255

CHADD
Children with Attention Deficit Disorders
1859 N. Pine Island Rd., Suite 195
Plantation, FL 33322
305-587-3700

The Attention Deficit Information
Network, Inc. (AD-IN)
475 Hillside Avenue
Needham, MA 02194
617-455-9895

ERIC
Clearinghouse on Disabilities and Gifted Education
Council for Exceptional Children
1920 Association Drive
Reston, VA 22091-1589
703-620-3660

National Information Center
for Children and Youth with Disabilities
P.O. Box 1492
Washington, D.C. 20013
703-893-6061

Parents of Gifted/LD Children, Inc.
622 Broad Street
Bethesda, MD 20816
301-986-1422

State Department of Education
(Call your State Department of Education
in your state capital and talk to the
Director of Special Education.)

U.S. Department of Education
Office of Special Education and Rehabilitative Services
Clearinghouse on Disability Information
330 C Street SW
Room 3132
Washington, D.C. 20202-2524
202-205-8241